AMERICAE, sive India Occidentalis pars.

Satyrorum inf:

Mare Cin

Campu

Inf. de Miaco

Torza   Saendeber

Chela

Miaco

academia   Bandu

Dalai

Homa   Amaguco

IAPAN.

Menlu   Malao

Hormar   Negru

Cangoxina   Frason

Hanc insulam M. Paul.

Venet Zipangri vocat.

Liampo opp.

et præf:

Chequeam

Mazacar

Cieuie

Tiguex

OCEANVS

Los dos hermanos

Lequio

maior

va Fermosa

Reix magos

Los Bolcanes.

Benfatera

insula.

Lequio minor

Tropicus Cancri   Lalabrigo

ORIENTALIS   La furfana

Baia de

innocentes.

Pauao:

das   Hanhan

Enilon.   Restinga de

ladrones.

Aguada   Humunu vel ya

di buoni segni.

Zamal

Catarain   Culuan   Cenalo.

Philippina   Hibusson   ARCHIPELA:

Abarien.   Huinangan   GO DIS.

Pasaie de S. Clara   Los iardines.

Paulogon   Calagan   ya de mata:

lotes

Cimbubon   va de arrecifes

Chippit   Mindanao.   LAZA:

Lozon   Buran   RO.

Infulæ Moluccæ, celebres ob maxima

aromatum copiam, quam per

totum terraru orbem trans

ferunt, s. funt, iuxta Gilolo

nempe, Tarenate, Tidore,

Motir, Machia et Bachia.

Candigar

Cabino   Ma:Talao, alijs Tarrao infule

Zolo.   Sanguin   Doy

Bilalon   Morotay

Tarenate   Gilolo.

Calamba.   Siua   Mamen: Circulus æquinoctialis.   va de crespos.

Tubân   Celebes   Gilolo   180

Guebe   ya de los

nhreires

Macaee   Cainam

Pulola.

or

NOVA GVINEA

quam Andreas Corfalus Ter:

ram Piccinaculi appellare vi:

detur. An infula fit, an pars

continentis Auftralis incer:

EXPLORERS

Philip Wilkinson

KINGFISHER

NEW YORK

KINGFISHER
a Houghton Mifflin Company imprint
215 Park Avenue South
New York, New York 10003
www.houghtonmifflinbooks.com

First published in 2002
10 9 8 7 6 5 4 3 2 1

1TR/0602/GCUP/MA(MA)/140NMA

LIBRARY OF CONGRESS CATALOGING-IN-PUBLICATION DATA
has been applied for.

ISBN 0-7534-5452-1

Editor: Carron Brown
Coordinating Editor: Sarah Snavely
Senior Designer: Jane Tassie
Consultant: Shane Winser, Royal Geographical Society,
    London, England
Production Controller: Debbie Otter
DTP Manager: Nicky Studdart
Picture Research Manager: Jane Lambert
Picture Research Assistant: Rachael Swann
Artwork Archivists: Wendy Allison and Steve Robinson

Printed in China

The Publisher would like to thank the Royal
Geographical Society (with The Institute of British
Geographers) for their help and cooperation
in the production of this book.

Since its formation in 1830, the Royal Geographical
Society has sponsored and supported expeditions
and fieldwork throughout the world. Today it is
at the forefront of geographical research and
education. The Society's Expedition Advisory
Center provides information, training, and advice
to hundreds of expeditions and field research
projects each year.

Further information about the Society can
be obtained from its website: www.rgs.org

CONTENTS

BEING AN EXPLORER

People have been traveling into the unknown in search of new knowledge for centuries—these men and women are called explorers. Early explorers traveled for all kinds of different reasons—to find new places to farm and settle, to claim lands for their rulers, to spread religions, or to make money. It was often dangerous work. They set off to places that had not been mapped, where the weather was unpredictable, and where they might encounter hostile people. Modern explorers mostly travel for scientific reasons, in order to better understand the world we live in. They can use the help of improved technology, but they need to be just as resourceful as their ancestors. The biggest physical challenges are in the most remote areas of the world—the polar ice caps, the deepest oceans, and even space—where explorers need to be well prepared, properly equipped, and brave.

Well equipped
Expeditions can take years to plan. Explorers have to raise money, gather together a team of people, and find the right equipment. A major expedition might require a huge amount of equipment, from vehicles and tents to medical supplies, fuel, food, clothing, and the items needed for research to be carried out. Everything has to be carefully chosen and tested before the expedition sets off.

Stranded!

Whatever the reason for exploration, going where no one has gone before requires commitment and resourcefulness. In the past polar explorers did not even have a radio to summon help if stranded—they could only use what they had with them and what they could find to help them survive. But even with today's hi-tech equipment, explorers still need these qualities when they venture out into new environments.

Fire starting

Making a fire has always been one of the most important survival skills. Fire gives us warmth and provides heat for cooking. A modern explorer might carry several aids to start a fire—waterproof matches, a flint and piece of steel to make sparks, and a magnifying glass to focus the sun's powerful rays on one spot, heating it up until it is so hot that it starts burning.

Could you be an explorer?

To be an explorer you need to feel at home in the outdoors and eventually you have to learn skills such as map reading, setting up and living in a camp, and first aid. The easiest way to start is to take part in organized outdoor activities through your school or local youth organization. As you do this you will begin to realize that there are many qualities you need to play a part in a successful expedition. You will need to be able to plan, research, and be a good team player. But if you can do these things, finding and sharing new knowledge is one of the most rewarding of human activities. When you are ready to venture farther, you will find many organizations that are willing to give you advice and point you in the right direction.

Preparation and survival

Explorers travel through unknown and often difficult terrains. They can face many different dangers, and help may be far away. To survive harsh conditions, explorers have to be prepared and equipped for survival. The expedition leader needs to pick a balanced team with a range of abilities and experience within the group, such as medical skills and experience of the terrain. To have the best chance of success, each team member needs to do plenty of research to find out all they can about the conditions they are likely to encounter.

Climbing toward the canopy
Jungle trees grow tall, their branches and leaves forming a high, dense layer called the canopy. This is where the majority of the rain forest wildlife lives and plants flower and fruit. To study the canopy, explorers climb the trees using ropes, aluminum ladders, and the knowledge of local climbers.

In the wet
Rain forests are the most humid places on earth, so the jungle traveler has to get used to being wet most of the time. But jungle travelers do not usually wear waterproof clothing—it tends to keep in the heat and just makes the wearer sweaty and uncomfortable. Tough, lightweight clothes that can be washed and dried quickly are best in this kind of environment.

Measuring up
These scientists are surveying an area of cleared rain forest in Brazil. The plants are growing back to form dense, secondary jungle. This thick forest vegetation is very difficult to travel through and explore.

In the rain forest

Tropical rain forests are a challenging environment for explorers. They are hot, sticky, dark, and noisy. The thick vegetation blocks out a lot of light, making the forest floor dark. Finding your way through dense undergrowth can be a slow, exhausting job. Deep rivers that are difficult and dangerous to cross, stinging insects, and diseases like malaria are additional hazards. But the jungle habitat is incredibly diverse, with thousands of different species living close together, making this one of the most rewarding environments to explore.

Forest in Brunei

Scientists on the 1991–1992 Brunei Rain Forest Project look at the forest from their boats. A team of 90 scientists studied a large area of forest—much of it undisturbed by humans—and took part in a variety of botanical, zoological, and geographical projects.

Habitat under threat

The world's rain forests are shrinking, largely because local people rely on the timber industry for their income. Explorers play a vital role in studying, recording, and protecting these important habitats. Because of their work, we now know far more about the jungle, and many useful discoveries are being made—from new animal species to types of plants that can be used in medicines.

Antarctic camp

These polar explorers have made a camp in the snow. They are setting up a Global Positioning System (GPS) that links to satellites orbiting earth in order to get an accurate reading of their position. There are no signs and few landmarks in the polar regions to guide explorers.

Polar exploration

In the polar regions—the Arctic and Antarctic—explorers have to cope with some of the most difficult conditions of all. Temperatures regularly go below −58°F (−50°C), and howling winds create severe blizzards. Anyone traveling in the polar regions needs to wear the right clothes. Polar explorers wear several layers of clothing covering their entire body but that allow good ventilation and at the same time keep in warmth. It is also vital to travel lightly and be able to move around easily in these harsh conditions. Glaciers, snowdrifts, and deep crevasses make moving around especially difficult—even with skis, snowmobiles, or sleds, progress is slow. Above all, the explorer must learn to respect this difficult terrain.

Desert exploration

There are several different types of deserts—some sandy, some rocky, others supporting scrubby vegetation—but they all have very low rainfall. Since there is no cloud cover, the temperature is boiling hot during the day and very cold at night. There can be virtually no water, shade, or shelter, and sandstorms are a problem in many deserts. Desert travelers wear strong, lightweight clothing that protects them from the sun and wind. Desert equipment also has to stand up to these harsh conditions. A good supply of drinking water is vital. Equally, desert explorers try to lose as little body fluid as possible, so they work in the evening when it is cooler and they are less likely to sweat.

In the sand

These scientists are analyzing desert soil and researching the plants that grow in it to find out more about desert habitats, which cover more than one third of earth's land surface. Reports on global warming suggest that temperatures are rising around the world, and more land will become desert.

Greenland

Empire and trade
For the Romans and other early people, there was often more than one reason to explore. While sending out cargo ships such as this one to expand their trade networks, they were also looking for new lands to conquer.

Brattahlid

EARLY EXPLORERS

NORTH AMERICA

Newfoundland

ATLANTIC OCEAN

People have always been exploring, fascinated by what is over the next hill or around the next headland. Our ancient Stone Age ancestors were constantly on the move, looking for new sources of food and new land to farm. By the time of the first great European civilizations, such as the ancient Greeks from the 400s B.C., people were traveling farther, finding places where they could start new colonies or find valuable goods to trade. Coastal people, such as the Phoenicians and Vikings, became great shipbuilders, and their vessels took them on long, often dangerous voyages around Europe and beyond to Africa and the Americas. But there were also noteworthy land explorers, travelers who braved the deserts of North Africa and Asia to find new routes, carry trade goods, and build alliances with far-flung groups.

SOUTH AMERICA

The Vikings in Greenland
Around A.D. 981 the Viking leader Erik the Red sailed west from Iceland, discovering Greenland. About four years later he returned to the island to live. The remains of one of his settlements, Brattahlid, can still be seen in southern Greenland. His son, Leif Eriksson, sailed to Newfoundland from here.

Iceland
(Thule?)

Shetland Islands
(Thule?)

Norway
(Thule?)

ASIA

EUROPE

CASPIAN SEA

Marseilles

BLACK SEA

Hindu Kush

Taklimakan
Desert

Beijing

Carthage

MEDITERRANEAN
SEA

BACTRIA

Xi'an
(Changan)

Tangier
Fez

Atlas Mountains

Baghdad

Bamian

Delhi

Marrakech

RED SEA

Timbuktu

Sahara Desert

Thebes

Mecca

Takedda

ARABIA

AFRICA

Calicut

PUNT?

Sri Lanka

Mombasa

Java

Australia

Key to explorers

——	Voyage to Punt 1492 B.C.	——	Chang Ch'ien 138–116 B.C.	——	Leif Eriksson circa A.D. 1000	——	Ibn Battuta 1330–46
-----	Hanno 470 B.C.	-------	Fa Hsien A.D. 399–414	------	Ibn Battuta 1325–27	---→	Ibn Battuta 1352–53
——	Pytheas 330 B.C.	——	Hsüan Tsang A.D. 629–645	-------	Ibn Battuta 1328–30		

11

Mediterranean traders and explorers

Greek explorers

The Greeks explored the coasts of the Aegean Sea where they set up colonies. In around 330 B.C., the explorer Pytheas sailed out from Marseilles, France, into the North Atlantic Ocean to a place he called Thule—perhaps Norway, Iceland, or the Shetland Islands.

The lands around the Mediterranean Sea were home to some of the greatest early civilizations, including the Egyptians, Greeks, Phoenicians, and Romans. Many of these groups settled by the sea and could travel more easily up and down the coasts than across the rocky, often mountainous, inland areas. They traded with people on the Mediterranean coasts and islands and then sailed farther in search of new customers, out into the cold, inhospitable waters of the Atlantic Ocean.

Phoenician travelers

The Phoenicians traded all around the Aegean, Mediterranean, and Black seas. Their most famous explorer was Hanno, who came from a colony in North Africa called Carthage. In 470 B.C., Hanno sailed far down the coast of West Africa where he found "a country smelling of spices from which fiery rivers fall into the sea, and the land is so hot that men are not able to go in it."

Phoenician ship

Murex shell

Trade goods

One of the most valuable Phoenician goods was the rare Tyrian purple dye made from a snail called the murex. Only rich people could afford the dye because hundreds of snails were needed to make even a small amount.

Ships of the Mediterranean

The Mediterranean explorers used wooden ships that usually had oars and square sails so that they could deal with all kinds of conditions—shallow and deep waters, and windy and calm weather. Ships were steered by a large oar in the stern.

On the march

In the 300s B.C. the Macedonians, under Alexander the Great, traveled over 20,000 mi. (32,000km) and carved out an empire that extended from Egypt to the borders of India. By A.D. 100 the Romans (shown above in Romania) had marched right across Europe, conquering most of the land between North Africa and Britain. They also made detailed surveys and built roads, providing greater access to huge areas of land.

Voyage to Punt

In 1492 B.C. the Egyptian queen Hatshepsut sent a fleet of ships on a voyage from the Red Sea to a country called Punt, which was probably in East Africa. When they returned from Punt, they brought back ivory, ebony, gold, spices, and creatures like baboons.

13

The Great Buddha of Bamian
On his route to India from China, the Buddhist traveler Hsüan Tsang reached Bamian, a religious center in what is present-day Afghanistan. Here he was amazed by the colossal gilded statue of the Buddha, 175 ft. (53m) high, cut into the cliff. He said that the statue was "glittering with gold that dazzled the eyes."

The empire of China

From 100 B.C. onward China had a huge empire that stretched from the Yellow Sea far west to the Yangtze River and beyond. Most of the big cities, such as Changan and Nanking, were in the east, and many travelers set out west from these centers. Some went to trade, some set out on diplomatic missions for the emperor, and others carried out religious quests.

Chang Ch'ien

The earliest-known Chinese explorer was Chang Ch'ien, who worked for the emperor Wu Ti. In 138 B.C. Wu Ti sent Chang on a long journey west to search for allies who would help him fight the nomadic people, such as the Huns, who were attacking the empire. Chang journeyed west but was captured by the Huns and imprisoned for ten years. Eventually he escaped and traveled to Bactria (northern Afghanistan). He did not find any allies, but he discovered a useful trade route that would eventually become known as the Silk Road.

The Hindu Kush
The Hindu Kush is a mountainous area in northwest Afghanistan. Travelers heading west or south from central Asia had to pass through the region, home to several groups of nomadic people. Both explorers and locals traveled through high mountain passes between desolate rocky slopes.

Buddhist explorers

Some of the greatest explorers were Buddhist monks and scholars, who traveled in search of relics, sacred sites, and religious books. Fa Hsien journeyed across central Asia and through northeast India before sailing to Sri Lanka in A.D. 399–414. In the mid 600s another Chinese Buddhist, Hsüan Tsang, traveled all around India, bringing home around 700 religious books and many statues of the Buddha.

The Taklimakan Desert
Both Fa Hsien and Hsüan Tsang had to cross this desert. It was a lonely place, and even today its rocky ground supports little life apart from camels. Fa Hsien followed a trail of human bones across the empty landscape, hoping that he would survive the crossing of this barren terrain.

Heavenly horse
In Ferghana (Uzbekistan), Chang Ch'ien admired the local horses, which the Chinese later imported. The emperor called them "celestial" (heavenly) horses, and Han sculptors made fine statues of them.

The Vikings

From their homelands in northern Europe the Vikings explored far and wide. From A.D. 700 there was a shortage of good farmland in Scandinavia, and people found it hard to make a living, so many Vikings took to their ships and explored. Some went raiding, stealing what they could from the people living in Europe's coastal villages. Other Vikings were peaceful explorers. They traded furs, whalebone, and walrus ivory and established new villages where they found land to farm.

Leif Eriksson

In around A.D. 1000 Leif Eriksson discovered a land he called Vinland, which was probably Newfoundland. He was one of the first Europeans to reach the Americas.

Compass

By lining up the needle with the sun at noon, Viking sailors could find out which way north was. They could then work out the direction they were sailing.

Iceland
The first Viking to settle in Iceland was Ingolf, who arrived in A.D. 870 in search of land to farm. Thousands of Vikings followed him in the late 800s and 900s. They built sturdy wooden houses that had no windows but had turf roofs to keep in the warmth.

Land ahoy!
A typical Viking ship had a large square sail, which gave it plenty of speed in good wind on an open sea. The sailors used oars when the wind dropped off or for rowing in shallow waters. These Vikings (below) are bringing their animals with them to settle in the new land.

Seafarers and settlers
The Vikings sailed along the coasts of western Europe and traveled far up rivers such as the Danube. But their most daring voyages were into the stormy, unknown waters of the North Atlantic Ocean. By around A.D. 1000 there were Vikings living in Great Britain, Ireland, Normandy, Italy, and Russia. In their search for new lands to settle on, they discovered Iceland, Greenland, and even North America. The east coast of America was so bleak that one Viking thought the whole coast "seemed to be covered with a single slab of rock."

Great ax
The ax was a favorite Viking weapon, but this one is so beautifully decorated that it was probably not used in war. A Viking chief would have carried it to show his great power.

By the 1300s, when Ibn Battuta was alive, caravans of camels regularly crossed the Sahara Desert, carrying salt and manufactured goods to important trading centers such as Timbuktu in Africa. Ibn Battuta joined a caravan when he journeyed east from Timbuktu.

Muslim travelers

The Islamic faith was first revealed to the prophet Mohammed in the Arabian peninsula in the 600s. Soon the followers of Islam, who are known as Muslims, were traveling far and wide, spreading their faith. Many Muslims were also merchants, so they had two powerful reasons for traveling—for religion and for trade. The greatest of all the early Muslim travelers was the explorer Ibn Battuta, who made land journeys through Arabia, western Asia, and India and sailed to China. But he is most famous for his travels across Africa's Sahara Desert. Toward the end of his life he wrote a book, *The Travels of Ibn Battuta*, describing his adventures.

On the water
Ibn Battuta used several different types of boats, including a canoe carved out from a tree trunk. At sea he traveled in a *dhow*, a slender vessel with triangular sails that was capable of sailing great distances.

Crossing the Sahara

Ibn Battuta traveled south from his home in Tangier, passing through the city of Fez, and journeying across the vast Sahara Desert. He faced sandstorms, snowstorms, and the Atlas Mountains on his way. Eventually he reached and explored the Niger River before arriving at the great trading city of Timbuktu. From here he headed east to another trading town, Takedda, before going north toward Fez. Along the way Ibn Battuta saw many wonders, such as a village of houses built from blocks of salt, and he observed many of the customs of the local people he met.

Muslim learning
Many Muslim scholars were experts in astronomy and navigation. This scholar is showing his pupils an astrolabe, an instrument used to measure the height of a star in order to work out one's latitude (distance from the equator). Muslim craft workers made the world's most accurate astrolabes.

Hippos on the Niger River
Ibn Battuta was fascinated when he saw hippos, but he could not have seen them too clearly because he wrote that they "have manes and tails, and their heads are like horses' heads."

THE SEARCH FOR TRADE ROUTES

From the Middle Ages more and more explorers tried to open up new trade routes. In Europe there was a huge demand for spices from Indonesia and materials, such as silk, from China. A few European travelers reached China by land, but many more tried to find the fastest sea route from Europe to the East. Some sailed around Africa, exploring the coast as they went. A few looked for shorter but more perilous routes through the icy Arctic Ocean. Other explorers, such as the navigator Christopher Columbus, sailed westward across the Atlantic Ocean, trying to reach China, but he discovered the Americas instead.

Alaska

Canada

NORTH AMERICA

Newfoundland

Hispaniola

Cuba

ATLANTIC OCEAN

SOUTH AMERICA

Strait of Magellan

Key to explorers

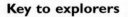

------- **Marco Polo 1271–95**

------- **Diogo Cão 1485–86**

------- **Christopher Columbus' 1st voyage 1492–93**

——— **John Cabot 1497**

——— **Vasco da Gama 1497–98**

——— **Christopher Columbus' 4th voyage 1502–04**

——— **Ferdinand Magellan 1519–21**

------- **Juan Sebastián del Cano 1521–22**

——— **Nils Nordenskjöld 1878–79**

——— **Roald Amundsen 1903–06**

Across Asia

One European who made the land crossing to China was Marco Polo, a Venetian merchant. Polo's account of his travels told of tall mountains, perilous roads, a variety of wildlife, and weird beasts with the bodies of men and the heads and tails of dogs. His descriptions inspired this illustrated map of Asia (right).

ARCTIC OCEAN

KARA SEA

Russia

ASIA

Bristol

BLACK SEA

Venice

BADAKSHAN

Gobi Desert

Beijing (Cambaluc)

Hindu Kush

Istanbul (Constantinople)

PACIFIC OCEAN

AFRICA

India

Philippines

Calicut

Cebu

Mariana Islands

INDIAN OCEAN

Indonesia

Mombasa

Cape Cross

Australia

Cape of Good Hope

The Silk Road

In ancient times the only people who knew how to make silk were the Chinese. Many people in Europe wanted to buy this luxurious cloth, and merchants from China brought silk all the way across Asia to sell in cities such as Constantinople (Istanbul) or Trebizond (Trabzon) on the Black Sea. The long route from China, across the Gobi Desert and through the mountains of the Hindu Kush, was called the Silk Road. Few Europeans were able to travel to China along the Silk Road until the 1200s, when the Mongols conquered central Asia. Soon after, merchants and missionaries braved the long and perilous journey.

The secret of silk
Silk workers spin thread from the material unraveled from silk moth cocoons. For centuries the Chinese told no one how they made silk. They could then charge high prices, knowing that European merchants could not get silk anywhere else.

At the court of Kublai Khan
Venetian merchants Niccolo Polo, his brother Maffeo, and son Marco visited Emperor Kublai Khan in Cambaluc (Beijing). Marco described the palace interior as "all ablaze with scarlet and green and blue and yellow." Niccolo introduced Marco as "your servant," and Kublai took him at his word. Marco worked for the emperor for 20 years.

The road to China
The Polos left their home city of Venice, Italy, in 1271. Most of the journey to China was by land. They rode on horseback, but their supplies were carried by camels and donkeys. The 5,000 mi. (8,000km) journey took over three years because Marco got sick—the Polos stayed in Badakshan, Afghanistan, for a year until he recovered.

The Franciscan friars
Some of the first Europeans to travel along the Silk Road were Franciscan friars, who went to Asia in the mid-1200s. One friar, William Rubruck, traveled in a covered wagon all the way to Karakorum, the court of the Mongol emperor. By the time he returned, he had covered some 11,000 mi. (17,700km).

A rocky road

The Silk Road was actually a collection of narrow, boulder-strewn tracks stretching across central Asia from Beijing, in China, to the Black Sea, on Turkey's border. It was a difficult route, crossing deserts and mountains, but China's merchants were prepared to take the risk, so it was busy with traders bringing rich goods to the West. They made sizable profits, as did the merchants who bought their goods. But few Europeans knew much about the Silk Road until the Polos returned. After they returned Marco was imprisoned by enemies from Genoa, Italy. He told a fellow prisoner named Rustichello all about his journeys, and Rustichello published a book called *The Travels of Marco Polo*. Some of Rustichello's stories were far-fetched, but they helped European traders access the Silk Road and discover the riches of the East.

Around the Cape of Good Hope

For much of the Middle Ages, Portugal was ruled by the Moors, Muslim people from North Africa. But in the 1400s the Portuguese reconquered their country and chased the Moors back to their African homeland. Portuguese sailors heard tales of great gold mines deep within Africa, and they began to navigate the African coast in search of riches. To begin with, seafarers such as Diogo Cão explored the shores and inlets of West Africa. They soon reached Africa's southernmost point, the Cape of Good Hope, and were on their way east to India.

The Cape of Good Hope
The rocky tip of South Africa was beaten by storms when Bartolomeu Dias and his crew sailed around it in 1488. Dias was the first to prove that a route to India around the tip of Africa was possible.

The Portuguese navigators

Portugal became a great sea power during the time of Prince Henry the Navigator (1394–1460), a noteworthy naval commander who paid for many expeditions. Henry's shipbuilders developed the caravel—a small, light, sailing ship that was ideal for exploration. Caravels could carry lateen (triangular) sails for coastal waters or square sails for the open seas. Portuguese navigators, such as Cão and Dias, sailed caravels. But the most successful Portuguese sailor was the trader and explorer Vasco da Gama. In 1497 da Gama sailed around the Cape of Good Hope and battled with storms and currents to sail up the coast of East Africa to Mombasa. He then crossed the Indian Ocean, becoming the first European to reach India by sea. Da Gama did not profit from trade with India, but he blazed a trail that was soon followed by other Portuguese traders.

Henry the Navigator
Prince Henry founded a school of navigation and built an observatory. His sailors rediscovered the Azores, the Madeira Islands, and the Cape Verde Islands.

Charting the oceans
Early mariners used maps called portolan charts. These were drawn on a grid of crisscrossing lines radiating out from compass points. The lines indicated compass bearings and helped show a sailor which bearing to follow. These charts were drawn on parchment paper made of goat- or sheepskin.

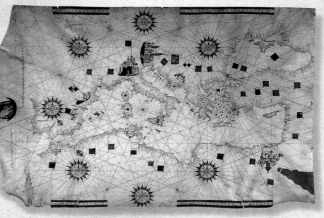

Along the coast
Diogo Cão looks at the African coast from the bow of his caravel. In 1485 he sailed all the way to Cape Cross on the coast of Namibia, much farther south than any previous European sailor and far beyond the edge of his chart.

The West Indies

Amerigo Vespucci
A businessman from Florence, Vespucci explored the east coast of South America in 1499–1500 and 1501–1502.

In the late 1400s European merchants became rich from trading spices from the islands they called the East Indies or Spice Islands (Indonesia). But the sea journey around Africa to the Indies was lengthy and dangerous, and they desired to find a quicker, easier route. Explorers such as Christopher Columbus, a sailor from Genoa, Italy, insisted that since the world was round, it should be possible to reach the Indies by sailing across the Atlantic Ocean. But no one knew that the Americas stood in the way. When Columbus sailed west in 1492, he discovered not the Indies but the islands of Cuba, San Salvador, and Hispaniola—what we now call the West Indies.

The American continent

Christopher Columbus and John Cabot, the explorers who crossed the Atlantic in this era, were convinced that they had discovered a group of islands off the east coast of China. But one explorer, Amerigo Vespucci, had a different view. Sailing far along the coast of Brazil, Vespucci realized that he had found not one of a group of islands but a landmass that was big enough to be a continent. Some experts believe that the name of the continent, America, is based on Vespucci's first name.

Claiming the Pacific
Vasco Núñez de Balboa, a Spaniard, crossed Panama in 1513 and was the first European to see the Pacific Ocean from the Americas. He claimed it for Spain.

Natural riches
Columbus wrote that the New World had "fine green trees, streams everywhere, and different kinds of fruit." Local plants such as pineapples and potatoes were unknown in Europe.

John Cabot
Sailing from the British port of Bristol in 1497, spice trader and navigator John Cabot crossed the North Atlantic and explored the coast of Newfoundland. The cod he brought back attracted fishermen to this coast.

The voyages of Columbus

Although Columbus was born in Italy, his expeditions were paid for by the king and queen of Spain—Ferdinand and Isabella—so Columbus claimed the islands he discovered for Spain. Columbus sailed to the West Indies four times. On his first journey he discovered Watling Island, Cuba, and Hispaniola. His second trip took him to Jamaica. On his third voyage he sailed via Trinidad to Hispaniola. He explored the Central American coast on his final trip.

The *Santa María*

Columbus' flagship on his first voyage, the *Santa María*, was only around 100 ft. (30m) long (barely large enough for a crew of about 40 men), but the vessel's square sails and sturdy timber took them all the way across the Atlantic.

Circling the globe

In September of 1522 a small ship, the *Victoria*, arrived in the harbor at Seville, Spain. The vessel and its tiny crew of 18 men were all that was left of a large, five-ship expedition begun by the navigator Ferdinand Magellan in 1519. It was the first ship to sail all the way around the world. The reason for Magellan's journey was trade. In 1494 a treaty had divided up the Atlantic Ocean and the lands on either side of it—Portugal was given the rights to trade in the East, Spain the West. However, who had the right to trade with the Spice Islands, halfway around the world, was in dispute. Magellan, sailing for Spain, set off west hoping to reach the Spice Islands via the Americas, and so he began the most amazing sea journey of his time.

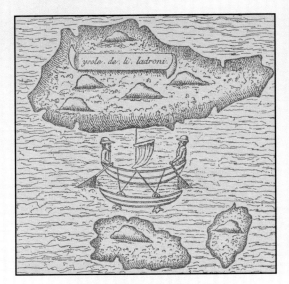

Pigafetta's book
We know about Magellan's expedition because of an Italian who sailed with him, Antonio Pigafetta. Pigafetta was one of the men who made it back to Europe. He wrote a book about the journey, *The First Voyage Around the Globe*, which was illustrated with maps and pictures of the ships.

The death of Magellan
After taking 100 days to cross the Pacific, Magellan arrived in the Mariana Islands, where he fought with the inhabitants after they stole one of his boats. He then sailed on to Cebu in the Philippines, where the people seemed more peaceful. The king of Cebu converted to Christianity and agreed to accept the rule of Spain. But many of the local people were unhappy about this and fought the Europeans. Magellan was wounded and died on the shore as his men ran back to their ships.

Magellan's expedition

After crossing the Atlantic, Magellan survived a mutiny, but one of his five ships was wrecked off of Patagonia. Then, while searching for a route into the Pacific, one of his ships deserted him and returned to Spain, but Magellan still found the strait leading into the ocean. The Pacific was larger than Magellan had thought, and they ran out of food. Pigafetta wrote that they ate rats, leather, and "old crackers, all full of worms." Many men died of starvation, and others were very sick by the time they reached the Philippines, where Magellan was killed. The remaining crew took two ships and sailed west to reach the Spice Islands in 1521. Only one of these, the *Victoria*, and its navigator, Juan Sebastián del Cano, finally braved the storms of the Indian Ocean to return to Spain in 1522.

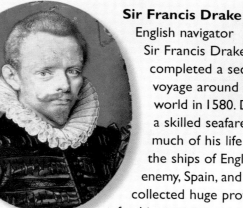

Sir Francis Drake
English navigator Sir Francis Drake completed a second voyage around the world in 1580. Drake, a skilled seafarer, spent much of his life raiding the ships of England's enemy, Spain, and collected huge profits for his sponsors.

Through the frozen north

Many northern Europeans thought that the fastest way to get to the East Indies would be to sail north. Several British expeditions tried to find a Northwest Passage to Asia through the frozen waters north of Canada, while sailors from Holland and Scandinavia searched for a Northeast Passage through the seas north of Russia. Neither group realized that the waters were just too icy to make the journey practical, and many explorers lost their lives in the search.

Franklin's goggles
From snow goggles to sleds,
Sir John Franklin was well equipped on his
ill-fated trip into the Northwest Passage.
These snow goggles are made
of leather and were worn to
protect the eyes from the
glare of bright sun
reflecting off
of the snow.

Nordenskjöld
Finnish scientist and explorer Nils Nordenskjöld made
it through the Northeast Passage between 1878 and 1879.
He knew he was likely to succeed when he sailed around
Cape Chelyuskin, the northernmost point in Asia and
a major stopover point on the way. He and his crew
put up a monument at the Cape to celebrate
their achievement.

Finding Passages to the East
The search for the Northwest Passage began
between 1400 and 1500, with explorers such
as the Bristol navigator John Cabot (see p. 26)
and the adventurer Martin Frobisher. Along with
later navigators such as Sir John Franklin, these
men found out a lot about the seas and lands
north of Canada. But it was not until 1903
to 1906, with the expedition of the Norwegian
explorer Roald Amundsen in his ship the *Gjöa*,
that anyone made it through the Northwest
Passage. The Northeast Passage also had
its pioneers, including the Russian Semyon
Dezhnev. Again success came to a Scandinavian,
Nils Nordenskjöld, whose triumph was due to
a lot of experience of Arctic waters and a ship,
the *Vega*, which had a special reinforced hull.

Willem Barents
Dutch navigator Willem Barents made several attempts
to find the Northeast Passage in the late 1500s. On his
last voyage in 1596 he rediscovered the island of Spitsbergen
before reaching the Kara Sea, where his ship became trapped
in the ice. Barents and his crew built a wooden hut for a
winter shelter. The following year they tried to sail back
to the Russian mainland in small boats, but Barents
died on the way.

To the North Pole by balloon
In 1897 the Swedish balloonist
Salomon-Auguste Andreé took off
from Spitsbergen for the North Pole.
His huge hydrogen balloon drifted
out of control for almost three days
before coming down. Andreé and
his two companions were forced
to leave the balloon's enclosed
gondola and continue the journey
on foot, dragging their equipment
on a sled. Three months later
they reached Franz Josef Land
but died before they could
be rescued. Their bodies—
and Andreé's expedition
journal—were found by
a scientific expedition
33 years later.

NEW HORIZONS

From the 1500s onward European countries began building up
huge empires in different parts of the world—Spain, France, and
Great Britain had colonies in the Americas, and the Dutch ruled large
parts of Southeast Asia. Several countries—Great Britain, France, Italy,
Germany, Portugal, Spain, and Belgium—took over areas of Africa.
Explorers traveled to all of these places, trading, settling, trying to
convert the local people to Christianity, or simply blazing a trail for
those who came after them. In the process Europeans learned about
some of the world's most spectacular places—from the lakes and
forests of Canada to the high Andes Mountains in South America.
Soon the search for new horizons took them even farther, and
they got to know the unique scenery and wildlife of Australia
and the inhospitable icy territories at the Poles.

Across Antarctica
In 2001 Ann Bancroft from the U.S. and
Liv Arnesen from Norway became the first
women to cross Antarctica on skis. The two
women pulled packs weighing around 550 lbs
(250kg) each on their 1,717 mi. (2,763km)
journey. The trek through subzero temperatures
and howling gales took 94 days. Most of the time
Bancroft and Arnesen traveled on their cross-
country skis, but when the wind was blowing
in the right direction, specially designed
parasails pulled them along.

The search for El Dorado

Many Spanish sailors visited Central America after Christopher Columbus' first voyage in 1492. They soon discovered that Mexico was home to an advanced civilization, the Aztecs, who built big cities and made beautiful jewelry out of gold and other precious metals. They also heard rumors of even more riches in South America and of a country so wealthy that their king's entire skin was covered in gold dust. This mythical figure was "El Dorado," and explorers soon set out to find his kingdom.

Exploring South America

——— Cortés 1519–21

------ Pizarro 1532

——— Almagro 1535–37

——— Orellana 1540

——— Valdivia 1541–47

Tenochtitlán

Quito

Cajamarca

Amazon River

Cuzco

Atacama Desert

Andes Mountains

Valdivia

Spanish explorers
Several of Pizarro's captains were noteworthy explorers. Francisco de Orellana followed the Amazon River, Diego de Almagro crossed the Atacama Desert, and Pedro de Valdivia marched south into Chile.

A king's ransom
Pizarro captured the Incan ruler, Atahuallpa, and the Incas brought thousands of gold objects for Atahuallpa's ransom. However, Pizarro did not release the ruler but had him killed after falsely accusing him of treachery.

Out with the idols
Both Cortés and Pizarro hoped to convert the people they conquered to Christianity, and Roman Catholic priests followed in the conquerors' footsteps. Cortés used this as an excuse to destroy many of the statues of the Aztec gods that decorated the temples in Mexico.

The conquistadores

Although they did not find El Dorado, Spanish conquerors—or conquistadores—quickly plundered the empires of the Aztecs in Mexico and the Incas of Peru. In Mexico the Spanish forces were led by the nobleman Hernán Cortés, who completed his conquest between 1519 and 1521 with help from some Mexican enemies of the Aztecs. Francisco Pizarro, with only 200 soldiers, conquered Peru in 1531 to 1533. In the major battle of Cajamarca, a peaceful meeting turned into a massacre when Pizarro's men attacked a horde of unarmed Incas.

The Aztec capital

Cortés was amazed by the splendor of Mexico's capital, Tenochtitlán. The capital, on the site of modern Mexico City, was in the middle of a huge lake. Cortés described a main square so large that "a town of five hundred people could easily be built within its walls."

Europeans in North America

Europeans who traveled to North America from the 1500s onward were amazed by the range of landscapes, from great lakes and fast-flowing rivers to high mountains and thick forests. To find their way European explorers learned about the country from the local people. Many travelers were fur trappers who followed local tracks and trails. Other pioneers, such as the French explorer Robert Cavelier de La Salle, kept to the lakes and rivers, using native-style canoes to find good trade routes. By the 1600s both Great Britain and France had set up colonies in Canada.

Across the lakes
French explorer Samuel de Champlain helped establish the French colony in Canada. With the help of native American guides, he explored the Atlantic coast and found a route inland by sailing up rivers to the Great Lakes.

Lewis and Clark
In 1803 the U.S. bought the vast territory of Louisiana from France. President Thomas Jefferson sent Meriwether Lewis and William Clark to explore the territory and find a route to the Pacific Ocean. Between 1804 and 1806 the pair canoed along the Missouri, Yellowstone, and Columbia rivers.

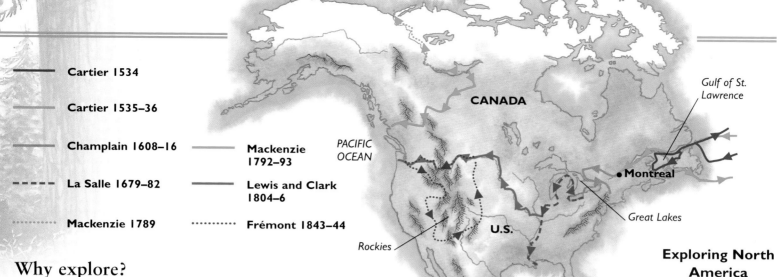

Exploring North America

Legend:
- Cartier 1534
- Cartier 1535–36
- Champlain 1608–16
- La Salle 1679–82
- Mackenzie 1789
- Mackenzie 1792–93
- Lewis and Clark 1804–6
- Frémont 1843–44

Map labels: CANADA, PACIFIC OCEAN, Gulf of St. Lawrence, Montreal, Great Lakes, Rockies, U.S.

Why explore?

People explored North America for many different reasons. Many of the first, including explorers in Canada such as Jacques Cartier, came to make their fortunes. They traded items such as furs, which could sell for good prices in Europe. Some came looking for land to farm and founded settlements that later grew into North America's great cities. Other explorers, such as the Scotsman Alexander Mackenzie, tried to find routes across the continent to the Pacific. Others were priests who hoped to convert native Americans to Christianity. Later pioneers pushed farther west, both to set up new settlements and to survey the land.

John Charles Frémont

Frémont was a surveyor who helped open up the western United States. He traveled the Oregon Trail and made many surveys that helped establish the boundaries of the U.S. Frémont planted an American flag on top of the Rockies, where he said the silence was complete, "unbroken by any sound."

Jacques Cartier

The French navigator Jacques Cartier explored the Gulf of St. Lawrence in 1534. Cartier, shown on this 16th-century map, returned the following year and sailed up the actual St. Lawrence River. He gave the name Mont Royal to the mountain that would later be the site of Montreal.

Crossing Africa

For Europeans and Americans in the 1700s Africa was a vast and mysterious continent. They knew it only as a source of slave labor, and they had only a vague idea about what the inland areas of Africa were like. Explorers in the 1800s, such as the German Heinrich Barth, who crossed the Sahara Desert, and the Britons Richard Burton and John Hanning Speke, who explored the Nile River, began to open European eyes to Africa. The best-known explorer of Africa was the Scottish missionary David Livingstone. He crossed southern Africa, following the courses of rivers and discovering several great lakes. He also spoke to Europeans about the evils of slavery.

Timbuktu
In 1828 the Frenchman René Caillié became the first European to return alive from Timbuktu and describe the fabled city. To get there he crossed the Sahara Desert from the coast of Guinea with a caravan of camels and traveled in disguise, wearing Arab clothing.

Speke's notebook

John Hanning Speke drew beautiful illustrations of the wildlife he saw on his journeys through East Africa.

At Victoria Falls

Explorer David Livingstone saw how the 5,250-ft. (1,600m-) wide Zambezi River plunged into a gap that was only about 65 ft. (20m) across. It created rushing, churning waters and great clouds of spray.

Victoria Falls

Livingstone traveled widely in southern Africa before making his famous journey across the continent in 1853 to 1856. Following the Zambezi River, Livingstone found the Victoria Falls and named them after Great Britain's queen. Leaving his canoe, he stood on an island in the river, watching the water plunge down over 330 ft. (100m). He later said: "Scenes so lovely must have been gazed upon by angels in their flight."

Richard Burton

Burton explored the Arabian Peninsula before setting off with Speke to search for the source of the Nile River in East Africa. The pair discovered Lake Tanganyika in 1858.

Exploring Africa

- – – – – – Caillié 1827–28
- ———— Barth 1850–55
- ———— Burton and Speke 1857–58
- ·············· Stanley 1871–72
- ———— Stanley 1874–77
- ———— Livingstone 1849–51
- ———— Livingstone 1853–56
- ———— Livingstone 1858–64

Exploring Africa

Although the explorers who went to Africa in the 1800s made noteworthy discoveries from the Sahara Desert to Cape Town, huge areas of Africa remained unexplored by outsiders.

Tripoli

Sahara Desert

Timbuktu

Lake Victoria

Congo

Lake Tanganyika

Lake Nyasa

Victoria Falls

Zambezi

Cape Town

Port Elizabeth

Pacific explorers

The Pacific is the world's largest ocean, but it was unknown to Europeans until Magellan's around-the-world voyage in the early 1500s. In the late 1500s and early 1600s, Spanish sailors Álvaro de Mendaña and Fernández de Quirós sailed to the Solomon Islands, the Cook Islands, and the New Hebrides. They hoped to find treasures, convert local people to Christianity, and set up Spanish settlements. Meanwhile the Dutch East India Company, based in Batavia (Jakarta), Indonesia, was also exploring the area. Dutch sailors brought back stories of a vast and mysterious land to the south, *Terra Australis Incognita*, or Great Southern Continent.

Keeping time
Cook was the first explorer to take an accurate timepiece on a long voyage. Knowing the exact time enabled Cook to work out his precise longitude, so Cook's maps and surveys were the most accurate of their era.

The South Pacific

In the 1700s British and French explorers searched the South Pacific for the Great Southern Continent. The man who finally solved the mystery was the British seafarer James Cook, who led three Pacific expeditions in the 1760s and 1770s. He first charted the two main islands of New Zealand and the whole of Australia's eastern coast, which would soon be settled by Europeans. He then sailed all the way around Antarctica and proved that the fabled continent was a vast, uninhabitable wilderness of rock and ice. Cook also discovered Hawaii on the way to finding an entrance to the Northwest Passage from the Bering Sea between Siberia and Alaska. Cook was famous for taking care of his crew, insisting that they eat plenty of fresh fruit to prevent the sailor's disease of scurvy, which was common at the time.

Louis Bougainville
Bougainville was a French sailor who explored the Pacific at the same time as Cook. His voyage around the world took him to Tahiti, the Solomon Islands, and the New Hebrides.

Cook and his team
Cook was one of the first scientific explorers. He took the naturalists Joseph Banks and Daniel Solander with him to collect and record everything they discovered. The artist Sydney Parkinson painted many of the plants they found. In one place they found so many new plants that Cook named the area Botany Bay.

Mapping Australia
The Dutch navigator Abel Tasman led two major Pacific expeditions between 1642 and 1643 on which he discovered Van Diemen's Land (Tasmania) and mapped large areas of the southwestern Pacific and the Australian coastline for the Dutch East India Company.

Crossing Australia

Australia's first settlers lived near the coasts of the country's southeastern corner. For years they did not go far inland because the hot, dry climate made travel difficult, and the Blue Mountains cut off settlements such as Sydney from the inland areas. By the 1820s explorers such as Charles Sturt were traveling along Australia's rivers, searching for new farmland. Soon after Europeans such as Edward Eyre, John Stuart, and Robert O'Hara Burke pushed still farther inland to explore the mysteries of Australia's dry, unwelcoming inland region.

John McDouall Stuart
John Stuart made several attempts to cross Australia. He finally reached the north coast, where he found a beach "covered with a soft blue mud" in July 1862.

Exploring Australia

· · · · · · · · · · · ·   **Sturt 1829–30**

————————   **Eyre 1840**

————————   **Sturt 1844–45**

- - - - - - - -   **Burke and Wills 1860–61**

————————   **Stuart 1861, 1862**

Darwin

Simpson Desert

Cooper's Creek

Blue Mountains

Adelaide

Sydney

Melbourne

Routes across the desert

Several explorers tried to cross Australia from south to north, hoping to win a prize offered by the South Australian government. One of the first was Edward Eyre, who got stuck in the salt lakes and had to abandon his expedition. Charles Sturt got farther, coming within 155 mi. (250km) of Australia's parched center. The first full crossing was by Robert O'Hara Burke and William Wills in 1860 to 1861. They used camels and set up camps along the way. Burke and Wills, with Charlie Gray and John King, made the full journey north, leaving the rest of their team at the Cooper's Creek camp. They hoped to meet up with the others on the way back.

Tragedy at Cooper's Creek

Gray died on the way, but Burke, Wills, and King made it back to Cooper's Creek. However, the other team members had already left. Burke and Wills were exhausted and died of starvation at the empty camp. Only King lived to tell the tale.

Australian wildlife
Europeans were fascinated by Australia's unique wildlife. Creatures such as kangaroos were also a valuable source of meat for explorers in the bush.

The ends of the earth

By the end of the 1800s the polar regions were still largely unexplored. Some ships had sailed close to the North Pole, and the Norwegian explorer Fridtjof Nansen got close in 1893 using sleds. An American team finally reached the North Pole in 1909. The South Pole, in the middle of the huge ice-bound continent of Antarctica, was an even bigger challenge. Glaciers, blinding snowstorms, shelves of ice, and howling winds held explorers back. In 1908 Irish explorer Ernest Shackleton led an expedition that got within 110 mi. (180km) of the Pole. In 1910 two expeditions, one led by the Briton Robert Scott and the other by the Norwegian Roald Amundsen, set off for the South Pole.

The _Fram_
Both Nansen and Amundsen sailed this ship. It was built with a reinforced hull so that it would not be damaged if the ship froze into the ice.

The North Pole at last!
American explorer and naturalist Robert Peary wanted more than anything to reach the North Pole. It was on his eighth Arctic expedition, in April 1909, that Peary claimed to have reached the Pole. His expedition was well prepared, and he had a large back-up team of Inuit, with many sleds and dogs. But people were suspicious; they thought that Peary could not have made the trip from his camp to the Pole and back to base in 16 days as he claimed. However, recent investigations appear to support Peary's claim.

The race to the South Pole

Both Scott and Amundsen wanted to be the first to the South Pole. Scott had already led one expedition to Antarctica, when he discovered Edward VII Land. Amundsen was also very experienced, having sailed the Northwest Passage. Amundsen originally intended to sail to the Arctic in 1910, but he changed his mind and went for the South Pole instead. The race was on. Both teams were well prepared, but Scott insisted on using ponies to pull the sleds. When the ponies died, he and his men had to pull their sleds to the Pole. It was slow work. In his journal Scott described "the soft snow clogging the skis and runners at every step, the sled groaning." Amundsen used dogs and was quicker. As a result Amundsen won the race on December 14, 1911. Scott arrived on January 17, 1912. He and all his men perished on the way back to their base.

Scott at Cape Evans
The British explorer set up a comfortable winter base at Cape Evans for his men. At his desk Scott kept a detailed journal and studied the results of the expedition's scientific work. Scott took several scientists with him, and they did important work recording weather patterns, collecting rock samples, and observing glaciers. They also studied Antarctica's most famous bird, the emperor penguin.

Dog power
Amundsen and his team traveled on sleds pulled by dogs, just as the Inuit did. The dogs served them well. For much of the journey they covered over 12 mi. (20km) per day, which is good going in the fierce, icy winds of Antarctica. Amundsen took care of his dogs, but he had to be ruthless. When they were near the South Pole, there were too many dogs to feed, and he ordered some of the animals to be killed.

EXPLORATION AND SCIENCE

Unlike previous explorers, most of whom voyaged to establish settlements or make their fortunes through trade, many explorers of the 1800s and 1900s traveled for scientific purposes—to observe new species of plants and animals and to examine rocks and fossils. Scientists on an expedition search for new knowledge and record everything they find. One of the most famous was the naturalist Charles Darwin, whose travels inspired and provided evidence for his theory of evolution. More recent explorers, such as those who dive into deep ocean trenches, make fascinating discoveries about life on our planet and the way different ecosystems work. Science, using new technology and inventions, also helps exploration and makes it safer. Whether they are using digital cameras, satellite navigation equipment, or the latest tough, lightweight climbing boots, explorers take advantage of the best that scientists and inventors can provide.

Core of the problem

Understanding climate changes can help us plan for the future. Antarctic scientists explore past variations in the weather by drilling out ice cores—long columns of ice from deep below the surface. The ice contains particles of dust and chemicals that can show how the climate has changed over hundreds and even thousands of years.

The *Kon-Tiki*

Norwegian archaeologist Thor Heyerdahl was fascinated by the similarities between the ancient cultures of South America and those of the Pacific islands. He wondered whether the people from Peru could have traveled to the South Seas. To test this theory, Heyerdahl built a balsa-wood raft, the *Kon-Tiki*, and sailed it 4,290 mi. (6,900km) from Peru to Polynesia. He showed that ancient navigators could have made the journey using the technology of ancient times.

In pursuit of knowledge

In the 1800s and 1900s naturalists traveled to many parts of the world, such as South America, Africa, and Southeast Asia, that were little known to Europeans. They were amazed by the thick forests and huge rivers and by the incredible variety of plants and animals. Richest of all were the tropical forests of South America, which hosted many explorers. The German Alexander von Humbold and Frenchman Aimé Bonpland traveled through the Andes Mountains. British naturalists Alfred Russel Wallace and Henry Bates explored the Amazon Basin. The most famous of the naturalists was the Briton Charles Darwin.

Darwin's finches
Darwin observed several different species of finches on the Galapagos Islands. The birds had developed different beaks to eat the foods available on different islands. The finches on one island developed thin beaks to spear bark-dwelling insects, while those on other islands developed broad beaks to crack open shellfish. The birds helped prove Darwin's theory of evolution.

Darwin at work
Charles Darwin was uncomfortable on board the ship. His quarters were cramped, and he suffered from seasickness. He still managed to fill many notebooks with his observations.

Humboldt in Ecuador
The German naturalist admires a volcano near Quito, Ecuador (above). In 1802 Humboldt climbed another volcano, Mount Chimborazo, reaching 19,030 ft. (5,800m), a world-record climb at the time.

Plant life
Bonpland drew thousands of plants, such as this *Inga excelsa*, which were unknown in Europe. Many of his drawings were published in Humboldt's huge 23-volume book about their travels.

Darwin and the *Beagle*

Darwin was only 23 years old in 1831 when he was given the job of scientist on board the *Beagle*. The ship sailed all the way around the world, but Darwin's most important work was done in South America and on the Galapagos Islands. Darwin was excited by what he found, especially in the rain forests. He discovered thousands of species and used his research to write his groundbreaking book about evolution, *On the Origin of Species*. In the Brazilian jungle Darwin was amazed by the noise of the millions of insects, which was "so loud that it may be heard even in a vessel anchored several hundred yards off the shore."

The route of the *Beagle*
The *Beagle* spent over three years of its voyage in the waters around South America before crossing the Pacific, Indian, and Atlantic oceans on its way back to Great Britain.

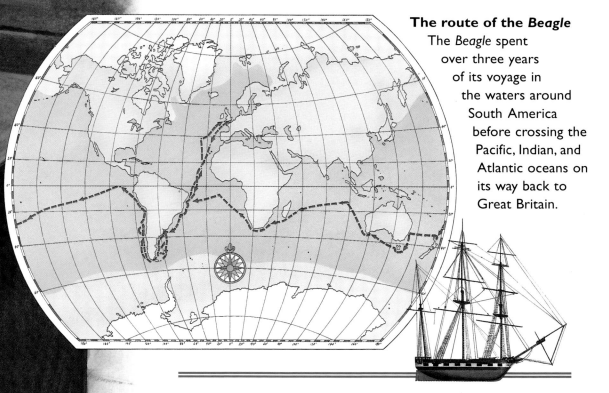

Scaling the peaks

People have been fascinated by the height and grandeur of mountain peaks for thousands of years, but climbing as a sport did not begin until the 1700s. The first mountaineers explored the European Alps, and by about 1870 they had scaled all the highest peaks in Europe. Since then climbers have traveled all over the world, mapping the world's greatest peaks. New equipment and a greater understanding of the effects of altitude on the human body meant that by the 1960s the world's highest peaks, above 26,250 ft. (8,000m), had been climbed.

Boots from Hillary's expedition
These leather boots from the 1950s were specifically made for the Mt. Everest expedition. They were light and held in the heat. Each boot had two layers of leather with opossum fur between the layers for warmth.

Conquering Mt. Everest
On Sir John Hunt's 1953 expedition New Zealand climber Edmund Hillary and Tenzing Norgay of Nepal were the first to climb to the top of Mt. Everest, at 29,030 ft. (8,848m) the world's highest peak. Their team used a camp at about 13,120 ft. (4,000m) to acclimatize themselves to the lack of oxygen. As they climbed they rested regularly to recover from the effects of the altitude.

Europe's highest mountain

In 1760 Horace-Bénédict de Saussure from Geneva, Switzerland, offered a prize for the first mountaineer to climb Mont Blanc in the Alps, the highest mountain in Europe. Frenchman Michel-Gabriel Paccard claimed the prize money in 1786. Saussure climbed the peak in 1787. He used ladders on the difficult descent.

Modern climbing boots

These boots are made from artificial fibers and plastic and are lightweight, warm, and waterproof. The materials also dry very quickly, which is important in icy temperatures when wet boots can freeze solid.

Everest, 1975

British climber Chris Bonington led an expedition up Mt. Everest in 1975. Taking the difficult southwest route, he and his team had to scale a perilous wall of ice on the mountain's face. On this occasion Bonington was not one of the climbers who reached the top. He achieved the summit on another climb in 1985.

Knowledge as a lifeline

Mountaineers need to be able to cope with high winds, steep rock faces, and worst of all, a lack of oxygen at high altitudes. The latest scientific knowledge and equipment have always helped. By the 1920s doctors had discovered that climbers needed to spend time getting used to high-altitude conditions in order to survive at such high levels without getting sick. By the time of the successful British Mt. Everest expedition in 1953, climbers had discovered that an extra oxygen supply at extreme altitudes improved their performance. They used the latest breathing apparatus, even though it was heavy and a burden to carry. Sir John Hunt, the expedition leader, said: "If not for oxygen, we would never have reached the top."

The ocean depths

Over two thirds of earth's surface is covered with water, but the ocean depths remain the least explored parts of the globe. This is because the sea is a dangerous place. To stay underwater for any length of time, people need breathing apparatus. For deep dives we need special equipment to protect us from the crushing pressure of the water. Because of this, scientists have only recently been able to study deep oceans. But the things divers have found, from bizarre deep-sea creatures to intriguing shipwrecks, have fascinated people all over the world.

Aqua-Lung
In 1943 the French scientist and filmmaker Jacques Cousteau invented the Aqua-Lung, a portable breathing apparatus that allowed him to dive without needing a link to the surface. Cousteau made dives all over the world using the Aqua-Lung, filming the incredible wildlife he saw. His device is now used by divers worldwide.

Deeper and deeper
Ocean explorers made deeper and deeper dives during the 1900s, but in the deepest ocean trenches the pressure was too great even for craft like the bathysphere. The breakthrough came in 1953 when Auguste Piccard, a Belgian inventor and diver, revealed his bathyscaphe—or deep-water vessel—the *Trieste*. In 1960 Piccard's son Jacques and American Naval Officer Don Walsh made the ultimate dive in the *Trieste II*—35,840 ft. (10,924m) to the bottom of the world's deepest trench, the Mariana Trench in the Pacific. Those onboard found a whole new world of remarkable deep-sea animals.

Beebe's bathysphere
The reinforced steel bathysphere ("deep ball") was designed by American diver Charles William Beebe in the 1930s. Its strong walls protected Beebe from the high pressure as he dived to depths of over 2,950 ft. (900m) off Bermuda.

Underwater helmet
Divers in the 1800s wore heavy metal helmets like this one, designed by the German inventor Augustus Siebe. A long tube linked the helmet to the surface, and air was pumped down the tube, enabling the diver to breathe. When the diver exhaled, the used air bubbled out through a pipe located beneath the neck.

Maps and mapping

Today we take maps for granted, but modern maps would not exist without the work of the explorers and surveyors who traveled into unknown territories and recorded the lay of the land. Ancient maps were not usually very accurate. There were many unknown areas, and mapmakers often resorted to guesswork to fill in the gaps. But as exploration increased and surveying techniques improved, maps became clearer, more accurate, and easier to use.

Dividers
Simple metal dividers have been used for centuries to measure distances on maps. By lining up the ends of the two arms with two points on the map and then moving them to the map's scale bar, the user can easily measure the distance between two places.

Ptolemy's world
Maps from the late 1400s were still based mainly on the *Geographia*, a book by the Egyptian-born Greek scholar Ptolemy, written in the A.D. 100s. He described the world of the ancient Greeks and Romans—Europe, West Asia, and North Africa. Almost everything else was *Terra incognita*, or unknown land.

The Renaissance world

By the 1500s the Renaissance, or revival of scholarship, had combined with the work of European explorers to improve world maps. This map benefits from the knowledge of Central and North America brought back by explorers such as Columbus, from the information about Africa provided by the Portuguese navigators, and from the data brought back by around-the-world sailors such as Drake and Del Cano. There are still huge gaps—little was known about South America, and the mapmaker has guessed the size of the legendary Great Southern Continent.

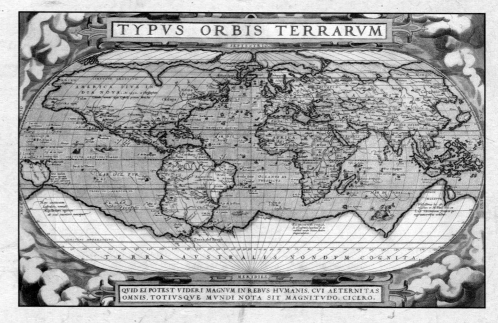

The story of mapmaking

Before 1600 most European world maps looked the same—they were based around the Mediterranean and often had Jerusalem in the center. But gradually maps improved as explorers discovered more about Africa, Asia, the Americas, and finally Australia. The growth of the printing industry in the 1500s also made maps easier to come by—before, each map had to be drawn by hand. In the 1700s surveying became more organized. The first national survey began in France, and surveyors traveled westward with the new immigrants to North America, mapping land available for settlement. By the 1800s surveys set new standards of accuracy. Some, such as the British Ordnance Survey (which began publishing maps in 1801) and the U.S. Geological Survey (begun in 1879), provided the ancestors of today's maps.

The 17th-century world

By the late-1600s the Dutch had sent their explorers into the southern Indian Ocean. Mapmakers were therefore able to chart large parts of Australia's coast, although they still thought it was part of a huge southern continent. On this map the mapmaker has avoided guesswork and left gaps in the Australian coastline.

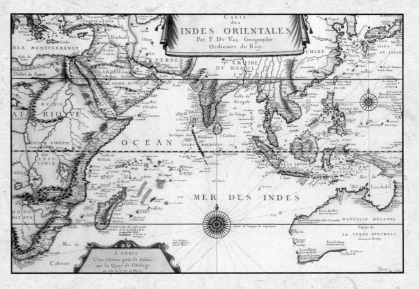

Piecing together a map

Piecing together a map

Nowadays the information used to put together a map can come from several different sources. A mapmaker may have a special survey done that measures distances and height on the ground and builds up accurate drawings from the results. Aerial photographs, taken from an aircraft with a camera pointing vertically down toward the ground, provide another source of information. In addition many of the satellites that orbit earth send signals that scientists can use to build up detailed pictures of the terrain.

Sextant

The sextant, invented in the 1700s, was used by explorers and surveyors to figure out their latitude. The user looked through the eyepiece and adjusted a moving bar until the sun seemed to line up with the horizon. A latitude measurement could then be seen on the curving scale at the bottom of the sextant.

Mapmaking decisions

There are many different types of maps—sea charts, town plans, territorial maps, and maps showing the features of the countryside—and a mapmaker has to decide what type is needed before starting to work. One of the main ways in which maps vary is in their scale—the relative size at which the features are shown. Small-scale maps do not show much detail but can include a large area, so a small scale is useful for maps of entire countries or even the world. Larger scales give more detail and so are used to show smaller areas. Many features are shown as symbols on maps— they can range from special marks to represent towns or buildings to colored shading for land at different heights above sea level. Maps also have a grid— the straight lines that help us figure out where we are on the map. These are often based on the lines of latitude and longitude that circle the earth.

Around and around

Globes are maps in three dimensions. A globe has one big advantage—if it is drawn correctly, all distances, areas, and heights can be almost exactly as they are on earth. This is impossible on a two-dimensional map.

Map projections

A projection is a way of depicting all or part of the three-dimensional globe on a two-dimensional map. There are many ways of doing this, and they produce very different results. Some projections, such as the one (right) devised by the 16th-century Dutch mapmaker Mercator, depicts all the compass bearings accurately and is ideal for navigators. Others, such as the zenithal projection (below right), show the surface areas of earth's landmasses in proportion and are used to calculate surface area, such as for maps showing land use.

Flying high

Satellites, carrying instruments that can detect the features on the planet below using infrared waves, produce detailed images that can be beamed back to earth. These images can show many types of things on the planet's surface—from buildings and vegetation to various types of rocks—and can then be used by a mapmaker.

Timeline

1492 B.C.
Queen Hatshepsut of Egypt sends an expedition to the land of Punt.

470 B.C.
Phoenician sailor Hanno explores Africa's north and west coasts.

330 B.C.
Pytheas, an explorer from Greece, sails to the northern land of Thule.

138 B.C.
Chang Ch'ien of China begins his long journey by land across Asia.

A.D. 629–645
Buddhist monk Hsüan Tsang travels west from China and explores India.

CIRCA A.D. 1000
Viking seafarer Leif Eriksson arrives in Newfoundland.

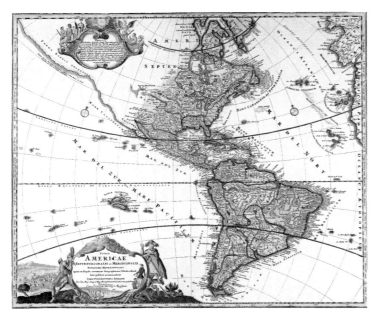

A.D. 1260
The Polo brothers, Maffeo and Niccolo, merchants from Venice, Italy, set off on a journey that takes them all the way to the Chinese capital, Cambaluc (Beijing).

A.D. 1352
Muslim traveler Ibn Battuta sets off on his journey across the Sahara Desert.

A.D. 1485–86
Diogo Cão of Portugal sails to Cape Cross on the Namibian coast.

A.D. 1487–88
Bartolomeu Dias becomes the first Portuguese navigator to sail around the Cape of Good Hope and reach the Indian Ocean.

A.D. 1492–93
Italian Christopher Columbus makes his first of four voyages across the Atlantic.

A.D. 1497
John Cabot sails from Bristol, England, across the Atlantic Ocean. He reaches Newfoundland before turning back.

A.D. 1497–98
Vasco da Gama of Portugal sails along the African coast and across the Indian Ocean to India.

A.D. 1519
Portuguese sailor Ferdinand Magellan begins his around-the-world voyage. He dies, but one ship makes it back to Spain in 1522 under Juan Sebastián del Cano.

A.D. 1519–21
Spaniard Hernán Cortés sails to, and conquers, Mexico.

A.D. 1531–33
Francisco Pizarro conquers the Incan Empire of Peru for Spain.

A.D. 1535–38
French sea captain Jacques Cartier explores Canada's St. Lawrence River.

A.D. 1539–42
Hernando de Soto from Spain conquers Florida and explores the Mississippi River region.

A.D. 1576
English navigator Martin Frobisher sails to Baffin Island in search of the Northwest Passage. He trades with Inuits and returns home.

A.D. 1577–80
Englishman Francis Drake sails around the world.

A.D. 1594–97
Dutchman Willem Barents leads three voyages to find the Northeast Passage.

A.D. 1603
French fur trader Samuel de Champlain arrives in North America. He becomes the founder of French Canada.

A.D. 1610–11
Searching for the Northwest Passage, Englishman Henry Hudson reaches Hudson Bay before dying in its icy waters.

A.D. 1642–43
Dutchman Abel Tasman explores the Pacific and makes the European discovery of Van Diemen's Land, New Zealand, and Fiji.

A.D. 1669–80
Robert Cavelier de la Salle, a French fur trader, explores Canada's Great Lakes.

A.D. 1690
Briton Edmund Halley invents the diving bell for underwater exploration.

A.D. 1766–69
Frenchman Louis Bougainville sails around the world and across the Pacific, visiting the Solomon Islands and the New Hebrides. The Great Barrier Reef prevents him from reaching Australia.

A.D. 1768–71
The British Navy sends James Cook on the first of his Pacific voyages of scientific discovery. He sails around New Zealand and navigates Australia's eastern coast, collecting many scientific specimens.

A.D. 1796
Scotsman Mungo Park explores the Niger River. He drowned on his second expedition in 1805.

A.D. 1799–1804
German scientist Humboldt and French naturalist Bonpland travel in South America, making many important scientific discoveries.

A.D. 1803
President Thomas Jefferson chooses Meriwether Lewis and William Clark to explore Louisiana, the territory that the U.S. had purchased from France.

A.D. 1828
Frenchman René Caillié, disguised in Arab clothing, visits the great trading city of Timbuktu in the Sahara Desert.

A.D. 1828–30
Charles Sturt explores rivers in south-eastern Australia, such as the Macquarie.

A.D. 1831–36
Charles Darwin, British naturalist on the around-the-world voyage of the *Beagle*, visits South America and the Galapagos Islands. What he saw helped him form his theory of evolution.

A.D. 1840–41
Edward John Eyre travels from Adelaide to Albany along Australia's southern coast.

A.D. 1844–46
Charles Sturt travels toward the center of Australia, proving that there is a desert in the middle of the continent.

A.D. 1845–47
John Franklin sails far west of Baffin Island before perishing, after his ship is trapped in the ice for 18 months.

A.D. 1848–52
Britons Alfred Russel Wallace and Henry Walter Bates explore the Amazon Basin.

A.D. 1850–55
German Heinrich Barth crosses the Sahara Desert from Tripoli to Kano.

A.D. 1857
Briton John Hanning Speke begins a series of expeditions in East Africa that lead to the discovery of Lake Victoria and the source of the Nile River.

A.D. 1860–61
Robert O'Hara Burke and William Wills make the land crossing from Australia's south to north coast.

A.D. 1871
Scotsman David Livingstone, on his fourth journey across southern Africa, is believed to be lost but is found by American Henry Morton Stanley.

A.D. 1872–76
The oceanographic exploration ship *HMS Challenger* undertakes a long voyage around the world. Scientists on board study every ocean except for the Arctic.

A.D. 1878–79
Swedish explorer Nils Nordenskjöld sails through the Northeast Passage.

A.D. 1893–96
Norwegian Fridtjof Nansen sails across the Arctic Ocean in the *Fram* and then sets off toward the North Pole on foot. He does not reach the Pole but gets closer than anyone has before.

A.D. 1903–06
Norwegian Roald Amundsen is the first person to sail the Northwest Passage.

A.D. 1908–09
Americans Robert Peary and Matthew Henson claim to reach the North Pole.

A.D. 1910–12
Roald Amundsen leads the first expedition to reach the South Pole.

A.D. 1910–12
Briton Robert Falcon Scott leads an expedition to Antarctica. Scott and his colleagues die on their return journey from the South Pole.

A.D. 1914–16
Irishman Ernest Shackleton tries to cross Antarctica from the Weddell Sea to the Ross Sea. He has to abandon ship.

A.D. 1934
American inventor Charles Beebe makes a record-breaking dive in his bathysphere.

A.D. 1943
French scientist Jacques Cousteau invents the Aqua-Lung, which makes underwater exploration easier and safer.

A.D. 1960
Frenchman Jacques Piccard descends nearly 36,090 ft. (11,000m) into the Mariana Trench in the bathyscaphe *Trieste*.

A.D. 1979–82
The Transglobe Expedition, led by Briton Ranulph Fiennes, follows the meridian around earth, crossing both poles.

A.D. 1993
Ranulph Fiennes and Dr. Michael Stroud make the first unsupported crossing of Antarctica on foot—1,350 mi. in 88 days.

A.D. 1999
Swiss pilot Bertrand Piccard and Briton Brian Jones are the first to fly a balloon, the *Breitling Orbiter*, nonstop around the world, climbing 36,090 ft. above earth.

A.D. 2001
American Ann Bancroft and Norwegian Liv Arnesen become the first women to cross Antarctica on skis.

Glossary

acclimatize To get used to a new climate or habitat.

allies People or countries who join in an alliance for mutual benefits.

altitude Height, usually above sea level.

analyze To carefully study the different parts of something.

archaeologist A person who studies the remains and monuments of ancient times.

barren Land that has no—or hardly any—vegetation growing on it.

bathysphere A round, deep-sea diving vessel lowered underwater by a cable.

bearing The direction of a place measured from a set point.

blizzards Storms in which heavy snow is combined with strong, cold winds.

botany The scientific study of plants.

bow The front of a ship.

bush Unsettled or uncultivated area of land covered with shrubs or trees.

caravan A number of travelers or traders traveling together overland.

cocoons The silky cases spun by insects, such as silkworms, that protect them during the period when they are changing into an adult.

colonies Settlements set up at some distance from, but usually still governed by, the people's original homeland.

conquistadores Spanish conquerors of Central and South America in the 1400s and 1500s.

continent One of the seven large landmasses of the world—Asia, Africa, Europe, Oceania, North America, South America, and Antarctica.

creek A stream or small river.

crevasses Deep cracks in the ice of a glacier.

ecosystem An entire environment, including an area, the living and nonliving things that inhabit it, and the interactions between them.

environment All the external surroundings in which a plant, animal, or human being lives; everything that affects its growth and well-being.

equator The imaginary line around earth, halfway between the poles.

evolution The development of a living or nonliving thing. Darwin's theory of evolution shows how all animals have evolved over millions of years into what they are today.

gilded Something that is covered with gold or a goldlike substance.

glaciers Rivers of ice that move very slowly down mountain slopes.

Global Positioning System (GPS) A navigation system that enables people to locate their position accurately by using radio signals from satellites.

globe Earth, or a map of earth, printed onto a ball.

gondola In air travel the capsule or container hanging beneath a balloon or airship that carries cargo or passengers.

habitat The natural home of a plant or animal, such as a desert, rain forest, ocean, or town.

headland An area of land that sticks out into the sea—a cape is a headland.

humid Moist or damp—used especially to describe climate or the moisture content of the air.

hydrogen A very light, colorless, flammable gas that is sometimes used to fill up balloons and was used in airships in the past.

import To bring goods into a country from abroad.

infrared waves Invisible waves of light that radiate out from earth's surface that can be used to monitor various geographical features from space.

jungle Forest in the tropical regions or near the equator with a thick growth of plants and trees.

latitude Distance north or south of the equator, measured in degrees.

longitude Distance east or west of the prime meridian, measured in degrees.

malaria Infectious disease spread by the bite of a certain type of mosquito that causes recurring chills and fevers.

merchants People who buy and sell goods in large quantities.

meridian An imaginary line around earth through both poles. Lines of longitude are measured east and west of the prime meridian, which runs through Greenwich in the U.K.

missionaries People who travel on behalf of a church or other religious body to preach and carry out community service.

native Belonging to a country.

naturalists Scientists who study animals, plants, or other aspects of the natural world.

orbit The path that a satellite or similar body follows as it circles around a planet.

parasails Parachute-like sails used to pull people on skis over the snow.

pioneers People who are the first to do something, such as the explorers who traveled into the uncharted land of North America to set up colonies.

polar At or near either of earth's poles; more loosely, in the Arctic or Antarctic regions of earth.

portolan chart A type of sea map used by early explorers on which compass bearings are shown as straight lines radiating from a number of points.

pressure The pushing force exerted by one body or substance on another.

rain forest Forest or jungle found in tropical areas; its typical features are dense vegetation and heavy rainfall.

runners Strips of metal or wood on which a sled slides.

snowmobiles Vehicles used for traveling across the snow; also known as skidoos.

specimens Items, such as plants, animals, or pieces of rock, collected by an explorer to show the typical features of an area or habitat.

stern The rear part of a ship.

strait A narrow channel of water linking two oceans or seas.

submersible An underwater vessel, such as a small submarine, that can work in water too deep for divers.

survey To measure and work out distances and heights in an area and then produce a map.

terrain An area of ground.

territory Land; an area of land owned by a country.

treaty A legal agreement between two countries or states.

trench A deep ditch or valley sometimes on the ocean floor, such as the Mariana Trench.

tropical In the tropics the region of earth marked by two lines of latitude—the Tropic of Cancer and the Tropic of Capricorn.

vegetation Plant growth.

ventilation The way of allowing fresh air into an area. Ventilated clothes allow excess heat to escape, keeping an explorer at a comfortable temperature.

navigate To travel by ship or boat or to plan the course of a journey.

navigator Person who navigates a ship; someone skilled in navigation.

New World The name given to the Americas by Europeans in the 1400s when explorers discovered the vast, previously unknown landmass.

nomadic Lifestyle that involves moving from place to place to find land and food.

satellites Objects that orbit earth or another planet.

scholars Educated people.

scurvy Disease caused by lack of Vitamin C, which makes the sufferer bleed underneath the skin.

secondary jungle Plant growth in a jungle that regrows after part of the forest has been cleared away; its typical feature is very thick plant growth near the forest floor.

Index

Acknowledgments

The publishers would like to thank the following illustrators for their contributions to this book:
b = bottom, c = center, l = left, t = top, m = middle
Nigel Chamberlain 50–51; **Gino D'Achille** 44–45; **Douglas Harken** 49 br; **Gary Hinks** 49 bc;
Adam Hook 12–13, 58 tl; **Richard Hook** 18–19, 28–29; **John James** 37 tr ; **Jack Keay** 22 cl; **Linden
Artists Ltd** 12 bl; **Kevin Maddison** 16 tc, 16 tr; **Salariya/Willii** 17 tl; **Mike Sanders** 37 t, 39 b, 42 c;
Claudia Saraceni 43 tr; **Thomas Trojev** 10 tl; **Richard Ward** 12 tl; **Mike White** cover, 8–9, 14–15, 24–25,
30–31, 32–33, 36–37, 40–41, 42–43, 46–47, 48–49; **Paul Wright** 34–35, 38–39.

The publishers would like to thank the following for supplying photographs for this book:
b = bottom, c = center, l = left, t = top, m = middle
Pages: **4** bl Corbis; **5** t Royal Geographical Society/J.T. Studley; **5** cl The Royal Geographical Society/Brunei
Rainforest Project 91–92/Chris Coldicott; **6** tl The Royal Geographical Society; **6** cr Raleigh International; **6** bl The
Royal Geographical Society; **7** cr The Royal Geographical Society; **10** bl Werner Forman Archive; **13** tr Ancient Art
& Architecture Collection/R. Sheridan; **15** tr The Royal Geographical Society/Ian MacWilliam; **15** cl Corbis; **15** br
Ancient Art & Architecture Collection/R. Sheridan; **17** cr Werner Forman Archive/National Museum, Copenhagen;
19 tr The Bridgeman Art Library/Topkapi Palace Museum, Istanbul, Turkey; **19** cr Bruce Coleman Collection/Joe
McDonald; **21** tr The Bridgeman Art Library/British Library, London, U.K.; **22** tl The Art Archive/Golestan Palace,
Teheran/Dagli Orti; **22–23** b The Art Archive/Bibliothéque Nationale, Paris, France; **23** tl The Master and Fellows
of Corpus Christi College, Cambridge, U.K.; **24** tr Art Directors & Trip Photographic Library/A. Tovy; **25** cr The
Art Archive/Naval Museum, Genoa/Dagli Orti; **26** tl The Bridgeman Art Library; **26** cr Corbis; **26** bl The
Bridgeman Art Library/Library of Congress, Washington D.C.; **28** tr The Bridgeman Art Library; **29** tr The
Bridgeman Art Library/Victoria & Albert Museum, London, U.K.; **31** tl British Library 10460.ee.15; **31** tr National
Maritime Museum Picture Library; **31** cr The Art Archive; **33** c yourexpedition.com; **34** bl AKG London; **37** cr The
Bridgeman Art Library/Brooklyn Museum of Art, New York; **37** bl AKG London; **38** bl The Art Archive/Musée des
Arts Africains et Océaniens/Dagli Orti; **39** tr The Royal Geographical Society; **39** cr Science & Society Photo
Library/National Museum of Photography, Film & TV; **40** tl National Maritime Museum Picture Library; **41** tr AKG
London; **41** cr The Art Archive; **42** tr The Art Archive; **44** bl Corbis; **45** tr Corbis; **46** cl Science Photo Library; **49** tl
The Art Archive/Navy Historical Service, Vincennes, France/Dagli Orti; **49** tr The Natural History Museum, London;
50 cr The Royal Geographical Society/Alfred Gregory; **51** tl The Art Archive/University Library, Geneva/Dagli Orti;
51 cl Chris Bonington Picture Library; **53** tl BBC Natural History Unit Picture Library; **53** cr Corbis; **53** bc Science
Photo Library; **54** tl Science Photo Library; **54–55** c Science & Society Picture Library; **55** tl The Art Archive/South
Australia Art Gallery; **56** br The Bridgeman Art Library; **57** cl Science Photo Library/GE Astro Space.

Every effort has been made to trace the copyright holders of the photographs.
The publishers apologize for any inconvenience caused.

Below is a list of useful websites:
www.rgs.org (The Royal Geographical Society)
www.raleigh.org.uk (Raleigh International, U.K.)
www.explorers.org (The Explorers Club)
www.nationalgeographic.com (National Geographic)
www.ses-explore.org (Scientific Exploration Society)

INDIAE ORIENTALIS, INSVLARVMQVE ADIACIENTIVM TYPVS.